CONST

For My Sons
Jeffrey and Donald
The new generation which will
cherish and defend the Constitution

13 14 15 16 17

Library of Congress Catalog Card Number 58-8398
Printed in the United States of America by
Polygraphic Company of America, Inc.

Bound by H. Wolff Book Mfg. Co., Inc.

Cloth covers printed by the Moffa Press, Inc.

The
First Book
Of The

ITUTION

By
Richard B. Morris

Pictures By
Leonard Everett Fisher

FRANKLIN WATTS, INC.
575 LEXINGTON AVENUE
NEW YORK 22, N. Y.

CONTENTS

THE STATES OR THE NATION?

In the late summer of 1780 a dashing young lieutenant colonel of the Patriot Army wrote a letter to James Duane, a member of the Continental Congress from New York. In his letter, the young man put down his thoughts about the nation. The War of the Revolution had dragged on for five bitter years. But this soldier was not afraid to look into the future and make plans for his country after the war was over.

The country was in a bad way. The government was too weak to give the Patriot Army proper support or to pay its bills. How could it get better and stronger? The young man's letter was very clear. Congress must have full power to act. It should have the right to tax. It should set up Cabinet officers who could manage affairs with foreign nations, the army, the navy, finance, and business. "There are epochs (times) in human affairs when *novelty* even is useful," the writer added. In this bold letter was a vision of the Constitution of the United States still seven years away.

The young soldier who wrote this remarkable letter was Alexander Hamilton. He was an aide to General George Washington. Soon he was to gain fame for his part in the capture of the British army at Yorktown. Perhaps because Hamilton had been born outside the United States, on an island of the British West Indies, he saw things more clearly than did many who had lived in this country all their lives. They were attached to their separate Thirteen States. Hamilton was attached to the Union.

Now, does it not seem strange that a brave people who had fought

GEORGE III

8

the powerful British Empire and were just about to win their independence had not yet found a way to govern themselves? On first thought it does, until we remind ourselves of the reasons why the Revolution began. The American Patriots had fought for freedom against a King and a powerful State. The State, they said, was made for man. Not man for the State. They then went ahead and of their own free will set up state governments and wrote state constitutions. But beyond this they were afraid to go. They were afraid to set up a national government to rule several million people who were spread out along 1,500 miles of seacoast and already were spilling over the Appalachian Mountains into Kentucky and Tennessee and onto the lands north of the Ohio River.

Such a big government seemed to many simple farmers, workers, and ordinary people to be a super-state which would crush their freedom. Remember that the Revolution had started because a central government back in England had tried to tax the colonies and to rule them more strictly. Would the people allow a central government here in America to do the very same thing?

It did not look as though they would. Of course, the Thirteen States had to act together to carry on the war. The way they did it was by sending delegates to a Continental Congress which met mostly in Philadelphia. This Congress was a revolutionary body. It first met in defiance of King George III of England. It appointed Washington commander-in-chief. It drew up the Declaration of Independence. It borrowed money from European nations, issued paper money, and carried on relations with foreign states. But this Congress was weak.

9

Its president merely presided over its sessions and had no power. Congress governed by committees. It did not have the power to tax. It could not force the states to pay the moneys needed to carry on the war.

THE NEW STATE CONSTITUTIONS

Just because the central government was weak does not mean that the people had not learned some things about governing themselves. In all the Thirteen States except two, the people through their leaders had drawn up written constitutions. Only in Connecticut and Rhode Island did the people keep their old charters, because they felt the charters gave them enough self-government. In Massachusetts the Constitution of 1780 was submitted to the voters. They accepted, or ratified, it. In other states the constitutions were framed by revolutionary congresses or conventions. These constitutions all said that they were based on the consent of the people. They provided for separation of powers — that is, the executive branch (the governor) was separated from the law-making branch (the legislature) and also from the judiciary (the courts). All but two constitutions provided for legislatures with two houses (bicameral). All provided for very weak governors, as the people remembered George III and did not want a return of tyranny, or harsh rule.

THE WEAK GOVERNMENT OF THE CONFEDERATION

The chief weakness was at the center. Congress took steps to set up a stronger government. A week after the Declaration of Independence was proclaimed, a first draft of the Articles of Confederation was put before Congress. But the war dragged on, and the Articles were not approved by all the states until 1781.

The Articles of Confederation was the first constitution for the United States. But it did not cure the real weakness at the center. It did not provide for a national union. It set up what was really a league or alliance of states. In Congress each state had one vote regardless of how big or how small it was. Congress did *not* have two very important powers — the power to tax and the power to regulate commerce, or trade. It lacked other powers, too. It did have the power to make treaties and declare war or peace, but for all important questions it had to secure the consent of nine states before it could act. To change the Articles of Confederation it was necessary to get the consent of *every* state.

The government of the Confederation was very weak indeed. It could not even pay its bills. It called on the states for the money it so badly needed. The states turned over only a fraction of what it asked. Congress named a remarkable financial genius, Robert Morris, to handle money matters. He had to admit that asking for money from the states was "like preaching to the dead." When Washington asked Morris for money for the soldiers, he said that it was as hard to pay them the money the country owed them as "to make bread of stones." Time after time proposals were made to place a tax or duty on goods imported into the country. But there was always one state that would block the tax. Even had they all agreed, the tax would not have provided enough money to meet the government's bills or feed and clothe the army. "A tub for the whale" was the way one Patriot described it.

At last England stopped fighting and America had won her freedom. But the new government was in worse trouble than before. The army had to be paid off. Some soldiers threatened to use force to get their back pay from Congress. A handful of troops mutinied, and forced Congress to flee from Philadelphia to Princeton. England had

Mutinous soldiers force Congress to flee from Philadelphia

13

L·E·F·

to be made to carry out the terms of the treaty which ended the war. By that treaty America was given a great area of land as far west as the Mississippi River and as far north as the Canadian boundary. But the British refused to give up their forts on the Great Lakes. They complained that America still treated the Tories harshly. These Tories were Americans who had taken the side of George III, and the British had tried to protect them in the treaty. The fact is that the British thought that America was so weak that they could continue to keep troops on American territory. There was nothing the new nation could do about it, the British felt.

All sorts of troubles among the states were arising at the end of the war. Many states had land claims in the West which conflicted with the claims of other states. Finally, all the states gave up these claims and turned them over to Congress. But before they did that, there was a great deal of bickering. New York claimed that Vermont was part of its territory and a war almost broke out between the two states. The people of Kentucky demanded independence from Virginia, and the people of Tennessee set up a separate state from North Carolina, which claimed their lands.

Debtors' prison

14

The end of the Revolutionary War saw an end to the business boom in the United States. Trade with the British Empire was no longer freely open to Americans, for they were no longer a part of that empire. The English dumped cheaply manufactured goods in America, and there was no tariff to protect our own factory owners and workmen. The United States had no power to control its foreign trade. To make matters worse, the states were taxing goods brought in from other states. Trade between states ground to a halt. Business slowed down. People found themselves out of jobs. Those who still had jobs were paid less wages, and farmers got much less for their crops. As conditions got worse, more people went into debt. In those days a man who could not pay his debts could be sent to jail or "sold" to work off the money he owed. Whatever price a man could sell his labor for would go to the man to whom he owed money. Soon the jails were crowded with debtors, and the auction block was a busy place as more and more poor people were auctioned off as servants.

15

Massachusetts was perhaps hardest hit. The farmers in the western part of the state were badly off and could not even pay their taxes. They said that if the state would issue more paper money they could pay off their debts. But the state legislature did nothing for them.

Suddenly angry crowds began to gather. Mobs prevented the courts from sitting. In this way judges would not be able to send debtors to jail. Finally, these desperate people took up arms under a leader named Daniel Shays, a farmer who was also in debt. The state of Massachusetts had to call out troops and use force to put down this uprising.

Shays' Rebellion, as it is now called, came as a fearful shock to America's leaders, to men like George Washington in Virginia and General Henry Knox of Massachusetts, who was Secretary of War under the Confederation. It showed what might happen unless a stronger central government was set up.

16

Shays' Rebellion

THE ANNAPOLIS CONVENTION

Just when the situation looked blackest, an able young lawyer from Virginia named James Madison got the legislature of his state to do something about it. The Virginians called for a meeting of commissioners from the various states to examine the regulation of commerce and to make certain changes (we call them "amendments") in the Articles of Confederation.

The commissioners met at Annapolis, the capital of Maryland, on September 11, 1786. Only five states sent commissioners to this meeting. They were New York, New Jersey, Pennsylvania, Delaware, and Virginia. The commissioners did only one thing that was important. In a report drawn up by Alexander Hamilton, they called for a meeting in Philadelphia to be held on the second Monday of May, 1787. The object of this meeting was to consider changing the Articles of Confederation. Congress approved the call for this convention.

The delegates arrive at the State House in Philadelphia

THE CONVENTION AT PHILADELPHIA

This was as important a gathering as any held in American history. No one said how the delegates were to be picked, but in every case the state legislatures picked them rather than the people themselves. And they picked very well, indeed. One of the members called the convention "the wisest council in the world." Many of the truly great men of that age were present. Americans now call them the Founding Fathers.

19

Virginia sent some of its very best men. The most famous of them was George Washington. But there were other big names, too. There was George Mason, who had drawn up Virginia's Bill of Rights, and Edmund Randolph, the governor of the state. And there was James Madison, thirty-seven years old, who had probably thought as much about what should be done as any American except Hamilton.

The Pennsylvania delegation was headed by Benjamin Franklin. He was eighty-one years old, but he had the wide-awake mind of a man of twenty-five. Franklin was a world-renowned scientist who had done more than any single man to bring France into the Revolution on the side of America. Above all, he was a very wise man.

There were other able men from Pennsylvania. There was Robert Morris, called the "Financier of the Revolution," the most famous businessman in the colonies. He was regarded as a wizard in money matters. With him came James Wilson, a skillful lawyer and scholar of government, and Gouverneur Morris, who was not related to Robert, but came from a rich New York family. Gouverneur Morris was witty and brilliant and moved around the floor of the Convention on a wooden leg.

New York sent the equally brilliant Alexander Hamilton, then in his early thirties. Along with him came two lesser men, Robert Yates and John Lansing, who were not in favor of a strong central government at all. They soon quit the Convention in disgust.

South Carolina sent a famous lawyer and planter, the fast-speaking John Rutledge, and the two Pinckneys, Charles Cotesworth, and his twenty-four-year-old cousin, Charles.

The small states also sent some notable men. William Livingston, the distinguished governor of New Jersey and a member of a famous New York family, was known as a fine writer rather than a speaker. Along with him came William Paterson, who had been born in Ireland and had made a name for himself as a lawyer and debater. Delaware sent the lawyer John Dickinson. On the eve of the American Revolution he had gained fame by denying the right of Parliament to tax the colonies. Dickinson was a true scholar, but not an exciting speaker.

From Connecticut came Roger Sherman, a self-made man, who had begun life as a shoemaker. He was awkward but very capable. William Samuel Johnson, the learned president of Columbia College, in New York, also represented Connecticut.

A number of these men later held high offices in the government. Two of them, Washington and Madison, became President. Two more, Charles Cotesworth Pinckney and Rufus King, delegate from Massachusetts, ran for the office of President. One of them, Oliver Ellsworth of Connecticut, later became Chief Justice of the United States.

In short, practically all of America's great men were present. Yes, there were a few who were absent. Thomas Jefferson was abroad as America's minister to France. John Adams was away from home as American minister to Great Britain. Patrick Henry, the famous orator ("give me liberty or give me death"), had been picked as a delegate from Virginia, but refused to serve. "I smelt a rat," he said.

He was afraid that there was a plot to take away the rights of the individual states.

George Washington opens the Philadelphia Convention

WASHINGTON AT THE HELM

The Convention started its first session in the Assembly Room of the old State House (now called Independence Hall) in Philadelphia. Uppermost in every delegate's mind was the question Franklin asked: Do we have the wisdom to govern ourselves? Before the sessions began Washington talked to the delegates. He urged them to work out a plan of government that would satisfy their consciences, that they could be honestly proud of. "Let us raise a standard to which the wise and honest can repair," he is reported to have said. "The event is in the hands of God."

The first thing the delegates did was to elect Washington as the presiding officer of the Convention. Then they picked William Jackson, a former army officer, for secretary, and decided on the rules to be followed. It was agreed that voting be by states. It was also agreed that a majority (more than half) of the states present could decide any question, and that each state, whether large or small, should have only one vote. This was a victory for the small states like Delaware.

23

An important rule of the Convention was that nothing spoken there was to be printed in the newspapers or talked about outside. The leaders felt that if the delegates could talk freely and exchange ideas with each other they might be willing to change their original ideas. They would be less likely to do so if what they had first said had gotten out to the people back in their home states. The Convention was strict about this rule of secrecy. One day a delegate dropped a copy of a report outside the closed door of the meeting. Someone picked it up and turned it over to Washington. He was very angry, and warned the delegates to be more careful in the future.

James Madison took a seat up front and kept careful records of everything that was said. Many, many years later, after everyone who was at the Convention had died, his account was published. Eight other members took some notes, but none were so careful as was Madison. Were it not for him we would never know what really went on behind those closed doors.

THE FIGHT BETWEEN THE LARGE AND SMALL STATES

The real struggle in the Convention shaped up at the start. Who would win out, the large states or the small states? Both groups had ideas about a new Constitution. Virginia, the biggest of the big states both in size and number of people at that time, already had drawn up a plan. It was presented to the Convention by Edmund Randolph. The small states in turn had a plan which was drawn up by William Paterson of New Jersey. There were other plans and ideas, such as those advanced by Alexander Hamilton, who wanted a very strong

James Madison records the debates

central government. These were considered too extreme and were not taken seriously.

Of all the plans, the Virginia Plan, the first to be presented, was the most important. It was the basis of the Constitution which was finally drawn up. This plan provided for a truly national government. Congress was to consist of two houses. The lower house was to be elected by the people. The upper house was to be picked by the lower house from persons named by the state legislatures. This Congress was to have the right to make laws "in all cases in which the separate States are incompetent." By this the Virginians meant in all cases where the states had no right to act. Under this plan Congress could examine all state laws and declare them illegal if they were against the Constitution or interfered with the powers of Congress. It also gave Congress the right to use force to carry out its powers.

The Virginia Plan provided for a president, called a National Executive. He would have all the executive powers that Congress had under the Confederation. He was to be chosen by Congress and to serve for a term of years. Together with a number of federal judges, he would have the right to veto the acts of Congress and examine the laws of the states. The Virginia Plan also proposed a system of federal courts to see that justice was maintained under law.

At once the Convention began to debate the Virginia Plan. First of all, at the suggestion of Gouverneur Morris, it was voted: "That a *national* government ought to be established consisting of a *supreme* Legislative, Executive, and Judiciary." This meant that the Convention had agreed to set up a supreme central government.

Now the small states were worried. Virginia had twelve times as many people as Delaware. If the lower house was to be elected by the people, and not by the states, the small states would be completely outvoted by a few big states. Things were moving too fast for the small states. It looked as though the Virginia Plan, with some changes, would be rammed through the Convention at top speed. At this point William Paterson proposed what is called the New Jersey Plan. This plan would have really continued the old Articles of Confederation, but Congress would have been given the right to tax and regulate commerce. Under this plan all states would be represented equally in Congress, regardless of their size, and the President would be under the control of the states.

THE GREAT COMPROMISE

The delegates debated bitterly. The New Jersey Plan was voted down by seven states to three. Then the Virginia Plan came up for a vote, and the small states rallied together to keep a super-state from being set up to rule over them. The fight was over whom Congress was to represent. Was it to represent the states or the people? Happily for the history of the United States, the men at the Convention were able to give a little to one side, and that side in turn was willing to give something to the other side. This is called a compromise. There were several compromises at the Convention.

The big one is known as The Great Compromise. Under this plan the lower house (House of Representatives) was elected by the people. This was a victory for the big states, who would have more seats than the small states. But the upper house (Senate) was elected by the state legislatures and each state would have the same number of Senators — two apiece regardless of size. This was a big gain for the small states. The Connecticut delegates had a lot to do with getting this agreement adopted, and so it is sometimes called the Connecticut Compromise.

Looking back over more than a century and a half that has passed since the Convention, it is plain to see that the small states had little reason to worry about the big states. The quarrels that were to take place would be between different sections of the country. For a long time before the American Civil War, the Senate was led by Southerners on such questions, and the House of Representatives by Northerners.

Practically everybody at the Convention took it for granted that there would be a legislature of *two* houses. Most of the colonies had two-house legislatures, copied from the House of Lords and the House of Commons of England. According to one story, Thomas Jefferson, on his return from France, asked Washington at breakfast why the Convention established the Senate. Washington asked him in turn: "Why did you pour that coffee into your saucer?"

"To cool it," Jefferson replied.

"Even so," Washington went on. "We pour legislation into the senatorial saucer to cool it."

By this Washington meant that the Founding Fathers felt that the Senate would be less likely to agree to extreme laws than the House of Representatives and would be less likely to go off half-cocked.

Who should have the right to vote for the members of the House of Representatives? That caused one of the great fights of the Convention. The first plan to be drawn up said, "the people of the several states," meaning those who could vote for representatives to the lower house of their state. Gouverneur Morris, the brilliant aristocrat, tried to bar anyone from voting who did not own land. He predicted that some day workers in factories would vote and he believed that to be dangerous. He felt that such people were ignorant and would vote the way the rich and powerful told them to. Fortunately the Convention defeated his proposals, and in this way showed its faith in *Government by the People,* what Americans call *Democracy.*

Gouverneur Morris

29

We the People

of the U...

...ure domestic Tranquility, provide for the common defence, pro...

...and our Posterity, do ordain and establish this Constitution for the...

In Convention Monda...

Pre...

The Sta...

New Hampshire, Massachusetts, Connecticut, ...Hamp...

Maryland, Virginia, North Carolina, South Carolina...

Resolved,

That the preceeding Constitution be laid by...

this Convention, that it should afterwards be submitted to a Convention...

tion of its Legislature, for their Assent and Ratification; and that ea...

to the United States in Congress assembled.

Resolved, That it is the Opinion of this Convention, that as soo...

United States in Congress assembled should fix a Day on which Elector...

Day on which the Electors should assemble to vote for the President, and...

That after such Publication the Electors should be appointed, and the...

fixed for the Election of the President, and should transmit their Votes c...

the United States in Congress assembled, that the Senators and Repre...

should appoint a President of the Senate, for the sole Purpose of receiving...

the Cong..., together with the President, should, without Delay, proceed...

D...k...on Secretary.

THE CONSTITUTION
Facsimiles of excerpts from the original document

...d States, in order to form a more perfect Union, establish just... the general Welfare, and secure these Blessings of Liberty to ourselves... ...ed States of America.

September 17th 1787

...nt

...f

...from New York, New Jersey, Pennsylvania, Delaware, ...Georgia

...he United States in Congress assembled, and that it is the Opinion of ...Delegates, chosen in each State by the People thereof, under the Recommend... ...ion or, assenting to, and ratifying the Same, should give Notice thereof...

...the Conventions of nine States shall have ratified this Constitution, th... ...ld be appointed by the States which shall have ratified the same, and a... ...ime and Place for commencing Proceedings under this Constitution... ...tors and Representatives elected: That the Electors should meet on the Day... ...id, signed, sealed and directed, as the Constitution requires, to the Secretary of... ...ives should convene at the Time and Place assigned; that the Senators... ...ing and counting the Votes for President; and, that after he shall be chosen, ...th this Constitution.

By the unanimous Order of the Convention
Go. Washington Presid.

LESSER BATTLES AT THE CONVENTION

The battle over Congress was the truly great fight of the Convention. There were other disputes, but they were rather quickly settled. Only three-fifths of the slaves, who were principally found in the Southern states, were counted in deciding how many representatives each state should have in Congress and how much it would have to pay in direct taxes. Congress was given the power to pass navigation acts (regulating shipping), which the North wanted. In return, Congress was forbidden from interfering with the importing of slaves from foreign lands for twenty years. This was done to satisfy South Carolina and Georgia. States like Virginia did not like the slave trade. Remember, the cotton gin was not invented by Eli Whitney until 1793, six years after the Convention met. In the year 1787 many Southerners felt that slavery was not profitable and was on its way out.

The framers of the Constitution provide us with a lesson in how to get along in club meetings, local and national gatherings, and even in international assemblages like the United Nations. One side cannot get everything. There has to be a give-and-take. For example, in the Convention some people wanted the members of the House of Representatives to be elected every year. Some felt they should serve for three years. They settled on two years.

Take the election of the President. Some delegates from the large states wanted the President elected directly by the people. But one delegate said that this would be as unnatural as asking a blind man to pick out colors. The small states wanted the President chosen by the state legislatures. So they compromised, and had the President elected by presidential electors, who in turn were elected by the people. Those who were more interested in keeping the states powerful than in building a strong central government were not at all happy about this. So the final draft of the Constitution left it up to the state legislatures to decide how the presidential electors were to be picked. The electors were to vote for two persons. The man receiving the greatest number of votes was to be President. The second highest was to be Vice President. But to be elected President one had to get a majority of all the electoral votes. If there was no majority for any one man, then the House of Representatives was to elect the President from among the top five candidates. Now, some men at the Convention wanted the Senate to have this power, because the Senate represented the states. They were afraid that in the House of Representatives three or four big states could get together and elect the President. So they compromised again. This time they agreed that the House was to vote for the President *by states,* and a majority of states was necessary to elect him. The House has elected a President on two occasions. In 1801 it chose Thomas Jefferson who was tied in electoral votes with Aaron Burr. Certainly it was a wise choice. And in 1825, when nobody had a majority, it picked John Quincy Adams instead of Andrew Jackson, who had to wait four years more to become President.

The decision to have the President chosen by electors was very important. It was a victory for the idea of a strong nation and, in the long run, for the people. Very soon nearly all the states decided to have the presidential electors chosen by the people instead of by the state legislatures. Another thing. Perhaps some people at the Convention had the idea that these electors would really use their own judgment and vote for whomsoever they pleased. Well, that idea soon gave way to the rule that the electors were to cast their ballots for the candidates for President and Vice President of *their party*. When the Convention met there were no real parties. Few people expected they would arise.

How long should the President serve? Opinions differed widely. Some men wanted a President for life. Some men were for a long term but without the right to run again. And again they compromised by fixing a four-year term with no limit on the President's right to run again. In fact, it was not until 1944, when Franklin Delano Roosevelt was elected for a fourth term, that a serious movement got under way to cut down the number of terms a President can serve. That movement resulted in the 22nd Amendment to the Constitution, limiting any President to two terms.

The Founding Fathers saw to it that in the new Constitution no one of the three distinct branches of the government (the executive, the legislature, and the judiciary) would become too powerful. Each one of these branches is protected from the other, and the people are protected against all of them. This is done through what we call Checks and Balances. The President can veto acts of Congress. Congress can impeach (remove from office after a trial) the President and the Supreme Court Justices. Although the Constitution did not expressly say so, the Supreme Court can declare an act of Congress void (no law) because it is against the Constitution.

Let us not get the impression that there was endless bickering, and

Chief Justice Charles Evans Hughes administers the oath of office to Franklin Delano Roosevelt, entering his 3rd term as President, 1941

that the delegates did not get the Constitution they really wanted. Just the opposite was the case. In general the delegates saw eye to eye. Both the Virginia and New Jersey plans granted to Congress the power to tax and to collect taxes. When the tax proposal was put to a vote, only one man in the Convention voted against it. The Convention unanimously granted to Congress the power to pay the debts and "provide for the common defense and general welfare of the United States."

Every plan proposed at the Convention granted to Congress the right to regulate commerce, both with foreign nations and between the states. This, too, was agreed to by everybody. The power to tax and the power over commerce were the two powers lacking in the old Articles of Confederation. Without them no government could be strong. A large majority of the delegates felt that the states should be forbidden to issue paper money, and the Constitution as finally written included such a restriction.

THE CONVENTION PERFORMED MIRACLES

When we think today of the endless debates that often go on in Congress over the passage of ordinary laws, it is a miracle that the Convention worked so fast. It all goes to show that the delegates knew that the need for a Constitution was urgent and that they mostly agreed on what should be done.

Just look at the timetable of the Convention. It first met on May 25, 1787. By July 26 the basic plan of the Constitution was agreed upon and referred to a Committee of Detail. That committee reported a draft of the Constitution, and the delegates debated the draft, clause by clause, from August 6 to September 10. On that day the Constitution was agreed upon and was referred to a Committee on Style to put it in proper literary form. That committee reported back *two days later*. It then took only two days more for the Convention to agree to the final Constitution. It adjourned on September 17.

Was not that a remarkable record for speed? We should take our hats off to the members of the Committee on Style who worked so fast and so well. They were gifted men and college graduates. Two came from Columbia, one was a Harvard man, another a Yale man, and a fifth was a Princeton graduate. They were Gouverneur Morris, who may have done most of the rewriting, ably assisted by Alexander Hamilton, Rufus King, William Samuel Johnson, and James Madison. Remember that *every single word* in the Constitution is important. And these men showed wonderful skill in picking words. What they turned out was a masterpiece.

A constitution is different from an ordinary law. It is not enough for a Convention to draw it up. It has to be approved by the people. That approval is called "ratification." Under the Articles of Confederation only Congress could propose changes in the Articles, and they would have to be approved by all the states. Otherwise they would not go into effect. You know how hard it is even in a small family or club to get every single person to agree on something. Practical people have learned that you have to act when *most* people rather than *all* people support you. So the delegates to the Constitutional Convention decided that the new Constitution would be submitted to state conventions for approval. If nine states approved or ratified, then the Constitution would go into effect. That turned out to be a very important and a very wise decision.

THE DELEGATES BID EACH OTHER GOODBYE

On the last day some of the great men spoke in favor of the Constitution. Alexander Hamilton, who wanted a stronger government even than the Virginia Plan, stood up and urged every member to sign the Constitution. Thirty-nine members put their signatures to the document. Only three who were present went home without signing.

Signing the Constitution

James Madison tells us that while the last members were signing the Constitution, old Benjamin Franklin looked toward the President's chair where George Washington was sitting. On the back of that chair was painted a sun. Nobody knew for sure whether it was a rising sun or a setting sun. "Now," said Franklin, "we know what it is. It is a rising sun."

Franklin was right. When the last delegate put his name on the Constitution, a new nation was established, one that was destined to become a great nation, and some day to be a leader of the free peoples of the world.

the Senators and Representatives before mentioned, and the
oath of the United States and of the several States, shall be bound by Oath or
required as a Qualification to any Office or public Trust under the United St

The Ratification of the Conventions of nine States, shall

so ratifying the Same.

The Word "the" being interlined between the seventh and
eighth Lines of the first Page, the Word "Thirty" being partly
written on an Erazure in the fifteenth Line of the first Page,
The words "is tried" being interlined between the thirty second
and thirty third Lines of the first Page and the Word "the" being
interlined between the forty third and forty fourth Lines of the
second Page.

Attest William Jackson Secretary

Article

done in Co

Day of September

of the Independa

We have hereunto

Delaware

Maryland

Virginia

North Carolina

South Carolina { Charles Cote
Charl
Piere

...bers of the several State Legislatures, and all executive and judicial officers,
...rmation, to support this Constitution; but no religious Test shall ever be

R. VII.

...fficient for the Establishment of this Constitution between the States

...tion by the Unanimous Consent of the States present the Seventeenth
...Year of our Lord one thousand seven hundred and Eighty seven and
...of the United States of America the Twelfth **In Witness** whereof
...cribed our Names,

...Fresh

...ing Bedford jun

...: Dickinson

...cd Bassett

...Broom

...cNenry

...S Tho. Jenifer

...arroll

...lair —

...son J

...OUNt

...Haight.

...iamson

...Hedge

...Pinckney

...inckney

...utti d

...w

...w

George Washington —Presid.t
and deputy from Virginia

New Hampshire { John Langdon
              { Nicholas Gilman

Massachusetts { Nathaniel Gorham
              { Rufus King

Connecticut { W.m Sam.l Johnson
            { Roger Sherman

New York ... Alexander Hamilton

New Jersey { Wil: Livingston
           { David Brearley.
           { W.m Paterson
           { Jona: Dayton

Pensylvania { B Franklin
            { Thomas Mifflin
            { Rob.t Morris
            { Geo. Clymer
            { Tho.s FitzSimons
            { Jared Ingersoll
            { James Wilson
            { Gouv Morris

THE GREAT FIGHT FOR RATIFICATION

Washington's diary tells us that after the last session the delegates "adjourned to the City Tavern, dined together and took a cordial leave of each other."

But they did not go home with the idea that their work was done. They knew that many people were afraid of the new Constitution and would try to prevent it from being ratified. In each of the states the Founding Fathers led the fight for the approval of the Constitution. Without them, it could not have gone into effect.

The Founding Fathers knew that they would have a hard fight, but they felt confident. They knew that the Constitution was so much better than the old Articles of Confederation that people would soon see that fact and favor it. The Constitution did correct the chief weak-

The delegates take leave of each other

nesses of the Articles. It gave Congress the power to tax and collect taxes. It gave Congress the power over commerce. It provided for federal courts and a strong President. It made the Constitution, the laws of the United States, and treaties with foreign countries the *Supreme Law of the Land*.

When the delegates got back home they found that some people did not like the Constitution or want any part of it. Politicians feared they would lose power if a strong national government was set up. People in the back-country, poor farmers and persons in debt, disliked the idea of too much government to start with. They thought the Constitution was an extra heavy dose. On the other hand, the businessmen, the workers in the towns, and most of the large landowners felt the Constitution would do them good and favored it.

43

It was the old Congress that really started the ball rolling. On September 28, 1787, that body sent the new Constitution to the states and asked the legislature of each state to submit it to a convention for approval or ratification. The movement to ratify started to snowball. First Delaware approved, and since then it has been called "The First State." Then Pennsylvania, New Jersey, Connecticut, and Georgia. By the time the Massachusetts convention met in January, five states had already ratified. In Massachusetts it looked as though the delegates who opposed the Constitution (they are often called Antifederalists) would win over those who favored it (the Federalists), but early in February that state approved by a close vote. It recommended some additions or amendments to the document. Most important, it urged that all powers not "expressly delegated" by the Constitution to the federal government be reserved to the states.

Then Maryland and South Carolina joined the parade. Now eight states had ratified and *only one more* was needed for the Constitution to go into effect. But at this point the enemies of the Constitution threw up a huge roadblock. The big fights were about to take place in Virginia and in New York.

On May 28, 1788, George Washington wrote to his friend and fellow soldier, the Marquis de Lafayette: "The plot thickens fast. A few short weeks will determine the political fate of America."

THE FIGHT IN VIRGINIA

Washington was absolutely right! The fate of America was not decided on the battlefield. It was decided in an assembly in Richmond,

44

George Washington writes to the Marquis de Lafayette: "The plot thickens fast!" →

Virginia, and a court house in Poughkeepsie, New York.

All the great supporters of the Constitution in Virginia attended the ratifying convention in Richmond. There was George Washington, James Madison, and the great cavalry officer, "Light Horse Harry" Lee, and John Marshall, one day to be a great Chief Justice of the Supreme Court. But they were opposed by strong men led by Patrick Henry and George Mason. Henry counted on Edmund Randolph, the governor of the state, to support his side. Randolph had left Philadelphia without signing the Constitution. But he stood up and said that he would no more consent to cutting off his own arm than to dissolving the union. That was the first defeat for the enemies of the Constitution.

But Patrick Henry was always a man to be reckoned with. He made a fiery speech attacking the Constitution as a threat to liberty. He said that he would rather have a King, Lords, and Commons than the new government. Henry warned that the happiness of one-half of the human race depended on what was decided. Just then a storm broke out, darkness closed in, thunder crashed, and lightning struck nearby. The session had to stop for a while.

Madison took up Henry's wild charges one by one. He showed that they had no basis in fact. When the vote was taken, those favoring the Constitution had won by a margin of 89 to 79. The Convention also proposed amendments to the Constitution, adding a Bill of Rights.

THE GREAT DEBATE IN NEW YORK

No struggle was more bitter than in New York. Those against the

Thunder and lightning interrupt Patrick Henry's fiery speech against the Constitution →

Constitution had a shrewd leader in Governor George Clinton. When the convention met at Poughkeepsie on June 17, two-thirds of the delegates whom the people had elected were opposed to the Constitution. Had a vote been taken then, it would have been defeated. But those who wanted the Constitution were against a quick vote. They felt that the delegates should think the matter over very carefully. "There are two to one against us," Hamilton said to a friend. "Tell the people of New York City," he added, "the Convention shall never rise until the Constitution is adopted." That meant keeping the pot simmering for six hot summer weeks.

The people who were against the Constitution had no plan of their own, nothing better to suggest. They knew, too, that the Constitution could go into effect when *nine states* had approved it. That would mean that the United States could get started without New York.

Those who favored the Constitution stood for *something*. Those against it stood for *nothing*. Back in the fall of '87 Alexander Hamilton got together with James Madison and John Jay, an important statesman from New York, soon to be Chief Justice of the United States. Together the three of them wrote a series of great letters, all signed *Publius*. For a long time who wrote each letter was a secret. They worked fast and furiously to get them to the newspapers. About two-

The Publius *letters appear in the newspapers*

thirds were written by Hamilton, but those written by Madison and Jay were also very important indeed. Before the Convention met at Poughkeepsie these letters which had been read in the newspapers were brought together in book form and were called *The Federalist Papers*. They are the clearest and ablest explanation of the Constitution that has ever been written. They were widely read and led many thoughtful people to feel that the Constitution should be approved.

The very first letter appeared in a New York newspaper on October 27, 1787. It stated that the author would appeal to reason and fair-mindedness. He would show that it was in the interest of the readers to back the Constitution, for the Constitution would assure them liberty, dignity, and happiness. Hamilton's last letter was written about a month before the New York Convention began. He urged his readers to approve the Constitution first and then seek to make changes or additions. He warned his readers that "a *nation* without a *national government*" is an "awful spectacle." He told them that adopting a Constitution in peacetime and by the free consent of the whole people would be a wonderful event, indeed. Nothing quite like it had ever happened before in history.

49

At the Poughkeepsie Convention Hamilton did most of the speaking for his side, helped by John Jay. A merchant and lawyer named Melancton Smith did most of the talking against the Constitution. The whole idea of a central government was too costly, Smith argued. It would let the government put its hands into the pockets of its citizens and give it too much power over their persons. Hamilton patiently answered him point by point. His speeches were among the most important ever to be made in the United States. He showed that it was not necessary to give up liberty in order to have union. He said that the states had no need to fear the new government. The people would see that the states would not be destroyed by any big central government.

While these debates were going on, news came that New Hampshire had approved the Constitution. This meant that nine states had voted for it, and the Constitution was already in effect. The enemies of the Constitution had built up a house of cards, and it quickly toppled. About a week later Colonel Livingston rode eighty-two miles on horseback from New York City to Poughkeepsie in about seven

hours with news that Virginia had also voted "Yes." What could the enemies of the Constitution in New York do now? They could only accept the Constitution outright or approve it and make certain changes in it. To everyone's surprise, Melancton Smith rose and said that he was won over by those who had spoken in favor of the Constitution. He told the delegates that New York should come into the Union with no strings attached. That settled it. A few others followed Smith. The Constitution was approved by the very narrow margin of 30 to 27. Here is one case where talking changed votes!

Now eleven states were in the Union, but the two still out were stubborn. In North Carolina they had to call a second convention before that state approved the Constitution in November, 1789. The federal government had already begun operations. Rhode Island did not even send a delegate to the Philadelphia Convention, so strong was the dislike of a strong central government on the part of its farmers. But this littlest state, more like a spangle than a star, finally came into the Union in May, 1790.

At last the original Thirteen States had formed a Union, and very soon two new ones joined. Vermont was admitted to the Union in 1791, and Kentucky in 1792. They had a perfectly legal right to come in, for the Constitution gave Congress the power to admit new states into the Union. Another thirty-three states were to follow them, until by 1912 there were forty-eight states.

Colonel Livingston speeds to Poughkeepsie with word that Virginia has voted "Yes"

THE PEOPLE CELEBRATE THE ADOPTION
OF THE NEW CONSTITUTION

All sorts of parades and pageants were given to celebrate the adoption of the Constitution. The most magnificent took place in New York City. The parade started at what is now City Hall Park. The most exciting float was a full-size frigate of thirty-two guns named the *Hamilton*. The parade moved down to Bowling Green and fired off a salute in honor of the President and the members of the old Congress,

Celebration!

then meeting in New York. There were sailors and ship carpenters on the floats, and tailors, upholsterers, brewers, and many other workmen marched along with them. They were all happy that the Constitution was soon to go into effect. Another huge parade was staged in Boston, and another in Philadelphia. There the bricklayers marched under the motto: BOTH BUILDINGS AND RULERS ARE THE WORKS OF OUR HANDS.

53

THE BILL OF RIGHTS

Parties and parades were not the whole story. There was still work to be done. Those who opposed the Constitution had shown that many honest men were worried that their liberties were not safe. A number of states approved the Constitution with the understanding that certain rights and freedoms would be added to the document as soon as possible.

The men at the Convention were just as much concerned about liberty as the men who were against the Constitution. But they felt that first things should come first. If there was no strong government, people would not be safe in their lives or property, and they would not be free. Congress could be trusted, they believed, to protect liberty.

Now the idea that people needed to be protected from their rulers by a bill of rights goes back a long time in English history. It goes back to the Great Charter, or Magna Charta, a great grant of liberties which the barons forced King John to sign in 1215. But in colonial times there was a very harsh king on the English throne named James II. So the English people overthrew him and made the new rulers, William and Mary, agree to a Bill of Rights which Parliament had drawn up.

At the start of the Revolution a number of states put such bills of rights into their constitutions. The first to do so was Virginia. These bills of rights forbade courts from imposing very high fines, or punishing a person cruelly or forcing a person accused of a crime to give evidence against himself. Some colonies even before the Revolution had protected religious freedom. As one writer put it, "To defend the

Christian religion is one thing, and to knock a man on the head for being of a different religion is another." The whole purpose of these bills of rights was to keep people from knocking other people on the head for what they said or what they believed.

Even the federal government had done something about the rights of its citizens. In 1787 Congress passed a famous law called the Northwest Territory Ordinance. This law governed the new lands north of the Ohio River and included a bill of rights protecting the people of this newly settled region from cruel and oppressive government.

So, you see, the idea of a bill of rights was not new at all.

Some members of the Constitutional Convention wanted a bill of rights. That is why the delegates put in provisions protecting persons from "bills of attainder" (laws punishing a person without a fair trial) and forbidding laws which declared acts to be crimes *after* they were committed. The Constitution also says that no man can be kept in jail without trial except in case of rebellion or invasion. But many people felt that the Constitution did not go far enough in protecting the people's freedom. The feeling was widespread. The Founding Fathers saw that the people would have to be reassured.

The new Congress which met in 1789 took action right away. James Madison proposed twelve amendments. Of these, ten were approved by the states and make up what we call the Bill of Rights or the First Ten Amendments. These became part of the Constitution in 1791.

The Bill of Rights tells the government just how far it can go. The federal government cannot require people to support a particular religion. It cannot interfere with religious freedom. It cannot interfere with freedom of speech. It must provide a fair trial. In recent times the Supreme Court has held that some of these guarantees or assurances of personal liberty also bind the states. They, too, cannot endanger personal liberties. The 10th Amendment protects the states and the people from the federal government. It provides that unless a power is given to the United States in the Constitution or denied to the states, it belongs to the states or to the people.

Freedom of religion

THE PRESIDENT AND THE CABINET

The Constitution provided for a President. He was given a great deal of power. He was commander-in-chief of the army and the navy. He could make treaties with foreign countries with the advice and consent of the Senate. He could appoint people to office and pardon offenders.

Nothing was said in the Constitution about the Cabinet, or body of advisers around the President. True, the President was given the power to appoint heads of departments and was allowed to ask them for written opinions. But that is as far as the Constitution went on the subject.

One of the first things that the new Congress did was to provide for these "Executive Departments" — the Department of State (or Foreign Affairs), the Treasury, and the War Department. Other departments were added from time to time. When Washington took office as the first President of the new government, he did not call these heads of departments together for regular meetings. He asked them to give him written opinions on questions. Alexander Hamilton, who was the Secretary of the Treasury, wrote opinions on almost every subject and came to have a great influence on Washington. Gradually, before the end of the first term, regular meetings of the department heads took place. Then the United States may be said to have had a Cabinet in the modern sense. Of course, no President is bound to take the Cabinet's advice. Under the Constitution he can do as he chooses, but most Presidents have listened to their Cabinets. The Cabinet and the Cabinet meeting are now regular parts of the way the President conducts his affairs.

THE SUPREME COURT AND THE FEDERAL COURTS

The Constitution provided for a Supreme Court and lesser United States courts, but was not clear as to how they should be made up. Congress set to work at once to correct this. It provided for a Supreme Court and a system of lower federal courts. More important, it stated that cases could be taken to the Supreme Court from state courts when there seemed to be a conflict between state law and the Constitution.

There was no question in anybody's mind that the Supreme Court could declare null and void (no law) a state law contrary to the Constitution. How about an act of Congress? Alexander Hamilton had the answer to that question in *The Federalist Papers*. He said that where Congress passed an act against the Constitution the Supreme Court could declare it void or "unconstitutional." That is just what Chief Justice Marshall did in a great case in 1803, known as *Marbury v. Madison*. Today nobody denies the right of the Supreme Court to pass on acts of Congress.

The Supreme Court

THE GREAT STRENGTH OF THE CONSTITUTION

Today people are seriously talking about making trips to the moon. When the Constitution was drawn up, it took three weary days to travel by stagecoach from New York to Philadelphia. Great changes have taken place since 1787. The United States of America is now a nation of 170 million people. It then had less than four million. The United States now extends from one end of the continent to the other and has military bases in many foreign lands. Americans throughout the world claim the protection of the Constitution.

That is the remarkable fact. Almost everything about the United States has changed, but the Constitution.

Nowhere else in modern times has a Constitution written by the people lasted so long. Most governments of the world have been almost constantly changing. There have been many revolutions. In some countries the head of the government barely stays in office a year. But

59

John Marshall

in the United States there is a Presidential election every four years and Congressional elections every second year. Any changes in government are orderly because they are in accord with the Constitution.

Why, then, has the Constitution lasted so long? Why is it still cherished by the American people? This is why they love it and will fight to defend it:

BECAUSE IT PROVIDES GOVERNMENT BY THE PEOPLE

BECAUSE IT PROVIDES FOR A GOVERNMENT THAT CAN ACT WHEN THE COUNTRY IS IN DANGER

BECAUSE IT PROVIDES FOR A FEDERAL UNION — where each state has powers in its own area and the national government rules in national matters. This keeps the government from getting too big and too far away from the people.

BECAUSE IT PROTECTS THE FREEDOM OF EACH PERSON EVEN FROM THE GOVERNMENT ITSELF

BECAUSE IT PROVIDES FOR A STABLE GOVERNMENT, one that is not easily upset.

BECAUSE IT HAS PRESERVED THE UNION.

The Constitution is a wonderful document, but its authors did not claim it was perfect. From time to time changes have been made in it. This is a right which the people have. But the changes have been *little* ones and the *big* Constitution has stood the test of time.

The Constitution stands for the nation and all the people who make it up. Whenever war or other dangers threaten them, they are determined, as was President Abraham Lincoln, "that government of the people, by the people, for the people, shall not perish from the earth."

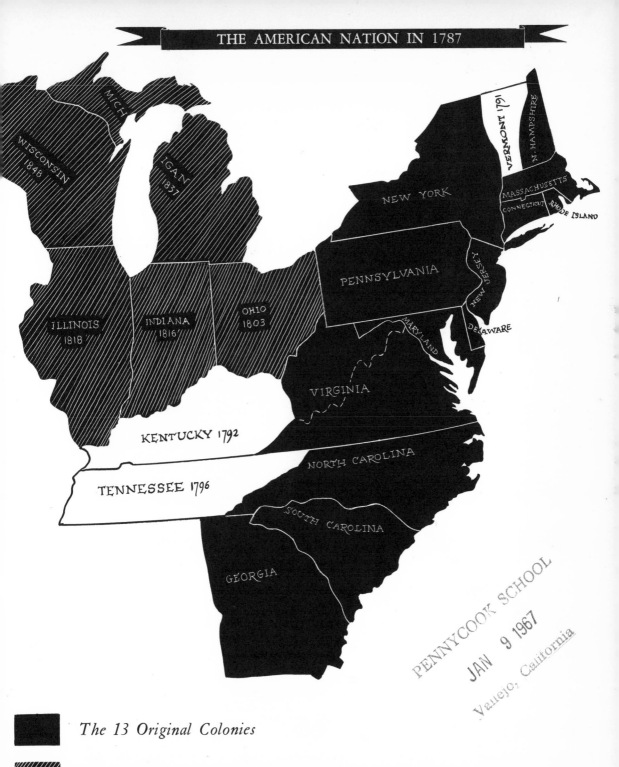

THE AMERICAN NATION IN 1787

WISCONSIN 1848

MICH

IGAN 1837

ILLINOIS 1818

INDIANA 1816

OHIO 1803

VERMONT 1791

N. HAMPSHIRE

NEW YORK

MASSACHUSETTS

CONNECTICUT

RHODE ISLAND

PENNSYLVANIA

NEW JERSEY

DELAWARE

MARYLAND

VIRGINIA

KENTUCKY 1792

TENNESSEE 1796

NORTH CAROLINA

SOUTH CAROLINA

GEORGIA

The 13 Original Colonies

The Northwest Territory   (Dates refer to time of admission to the Union)

THE CONSTITUTION OF THE UNITED STATES
A Simplified Outline

Preamble

"We the People of the United States, in order to form a more perfect union, establish justice, insure domestic tranquility, provide for the common defense, promote the general welfare, and secure the blessings of liberty to ourselves and our posterity, do ordain and establish this Constitution for the United States of America."

1. The Constitution gives the *power of making laws* to *Congress.*

   Congress shall consist of two houses, a *Senate* and a *House of Representatives.*

   The House of Representatives:

   Term of members: two years

A member must be at least twenty-five years old, seven years a citizen of the U. S., and when elected, an inhabitant of the state in which he was elected. Representation and direct taxes are decided according to the number of people living in each state. Originally persons not free (meaning Negro slaves) counted as three-fifths of free persons for those purposes, but since the *14th Amendment* this is no longer the case.

Not more than one representative for every thirty thousand people.

The House shall choose its Speaker and other officers.

The Senate

Term of senators: six years (one out of every three senators completes his term every two years).

A senator must be thirty years of age, nine years a citizen of the U. S., and an inhabitant of the state in which he was chosen.

The Vice President of the U. S. is President of the Senate, but only votes when there is a tie.

Privileges or Rights of Congress

Members cannot be arrested when attending sessions or going to or returning home. Members cannot be questioned in any other place for any speech or debate in either House.

Lawmaking

Money bills must start in the House. Then they have to be approved by the Senate.

When a bill passes both Houses it goes to the President for his approval. If he signs the bill it becomes law. If he does not want to sign it, he should return it to Congress, which can pass it over his *veto* by a two-thirds vote in both Houses. If the President does not return the bill in 10 days it becomes a law without his signature. But if Congress has already adjourned and he fails to return it, it is not a law *(pocket veto)*.

Powers of Congress

To lay and collect taxes

To pay the debts

To provide for the common defense and general welfare of the U. S.

To borrow money

To regulate commerce with foreign nations and among the states

To establish uniform rules of naturalization (making people not born in U. S. American citizens)

To coin money

To set up lower federal courts

To declare war

To raise and support an army and a navy

To provide for calling out the state militia to carry out the laws of the U. S., put down rebellion and repel invasions

To govern an area not to exceed ten miles square to become the Capital of the U. S. (This became Washington, D. C.), and to govern forts, arsenals, dockyards, and other "needful buildings"

To admit new states into the Union

To make rules and regulations for the territories of the U. S.

"To make all laws which shall be necessary and proper for carrying into execution the foregoing powers."

2. The Constitution gives the *"executive power"* to the *President.*

Term of the President is four years.

Election by an *electoral college.* The person having the greatest number of votes to be President; second highest, Vice President. In case no one has a majority of the electoral votes, then the House of Representatives shall pick a President from the top five. The House shall vote by states and a majority is needed to elect. The *12th Amendment* (1804) provided that the electors state who their choice was for President and who it was for Vice President.

A President must be "a natural born citizen" or a citizen of the U. S. at the time of the adoption of the Constitution. He must be at least thirty-five years old and a resident within the U. S. for fourteen years. The Vice President shall act as President in case the President is removed from office or is unable to carry on his duties, or in case he dies. Before entering office the President is required to take an oath to "preserve, protect, and defend the Constitution of the United States."

Powers of the President

He is commander-in-chief of the army and navy and of the state militia when called into the service of the U. S.

He may pardon persons punished for offenses against the U. S.

He can make treaties, but two-thirds of the Senators must agree to them.

He appoints public officials, ambassadors, Supreme Court judges, etc., with the advice and consent of the Senate.

He can call both Houses together on very special occasions.

He is to carry out the laws of the U. S. faithfully.

Removal:

The President, Vice President, and all other civil officials can be removed from office on impeachment for, and conviction of "treason, bribery, or other high crimes and misdemeanors." The House of Representatives presents the charges against the official, who is tried in the Senate. In an impeachment trial of the President the Chief Justice presides over the Senate and a two-thirds vote is necessary for conviction. No President has ever been convicted and only one (President Johnson) was ever tried.

3. The Constitution gives the "judicial power," the power of judging, to a *Supreme Court* and lower courts.

    Term of the judges: They shall hold office "during good behavior" — that is to say, they cannot be dismissed unless they do wrong.

    The U. S. courts can hear suits between states, between a state and a citizen of another state, between citizens of different states, and between a state or citizen and a foreign state or a foreign citizen. They can also try cases arising from matters on the high seas (admiralty).

    All crimes, except impeachment of officeholders, shall be tried by jury. Treason against the U. S. shall consist in making war or joining the enemies of the U. S. or "giving them aid and comfort." No person shall be convicted of treason unless two witnesses saw him commit the act, or unless he confesses in court.

4. The Constitution *forbids the states*

    To make a treaty or alliance with a foreign country

    To issue paper money

    To keep contracts from being carried out

    To grant titles of nobility (Congress also is not allowed to do this)

    To levy taxes on imports or exports

    To keep troops or ships of war in times of peace

    To go to war without the consent of Congress.

5. To change or amend the Constitution two ways are provided:

    a) Congress by a *two-thirds* vote can propose an amendment

    b) A Convention can be called by two-thirds of the states to propose amendments

    In either case, *three-fourths of the state legislatures* must approve the change before it becomes a part of the Constitution.

6. The Constitution, the laws of the U. S., and Treaties shall be "the supreme law of the land," binding on every judge in every state.

7. Nobody shall be required to belong to a particular religion in order to hold an office in the U. S. government.

THE AMENDMENTS

(Dates tell when the amendment became a part of the Constitution.)

The Bill of Rights (or *First Ten Amendments*) (1791)

1. Congress is forbidden to pass any law setting up a religion or interfering with religious freedom or with free speech or with the right of people to get together peacefully and petition the government to have their grievances looked into.

2. The right of the people to keep and bear arms shall not be interfered with.

3. No soldier in time of peace shall be assigned to live in a private home without the consent of the owner, nor in time of war except in a lawful manner.

4. The people are protected against search and seizure without a warrant.

5. A grand jury is provided for in serious crimes. Persons are protected from being tried twice for the same offense, or from having to testify in criminal cases against themselves, or from being deprived of life, liberty, or property without lawful means.

6. A fair and speedy trial for the accused is guaranteed in criminal cases.

7. A jury trial is provided for in civil suits exceeding $20.

8. Very high bail, stiff fines, or cruel punishment are forbidden.

9. Just because certain rights of the people have been stated in the Constitution does not mean that they do not have still others not mentioned there.

10. All powers not given by the Constitution to the U. S. nor forbidden to the states are reserved to the states or to the people.

11. Forbids the citizens of another state or of a foreign country from suing a state in the U. S. courts (1798).

12. Provides that the electors should state on their ballots the person they want for President and the person for Vice President (1804).

13. Forbids slavery and "involuntary servitude" (1865).

14. Forbids states from passing laws depriving *any* person of life, liberty, or property "without due process of law" or of not giving to each person the equal protection of the law (1868).

15. Forbids the U. S. or any state from preventing a person from voting because of "race, color, or previous condition of servitude" (1870).

16. Permits the income tax (1913).

17. Provides for the election of Senators *by the people* instead of by the state legislatures (1913).

18. Forbids the manufacture, sale or shipment of intoxicating liquors (the *Prohibition Amendment*) (1919).

19. Gives women the vote (1920).

20. The term of the President ends on January 20. If the President elect dies before his term begins, the Vice President elect shall become President (1933).

21. Repeals the 18th Amendment; once more allows the making and sale of liquor (1933).

22. Bars any President from serving more than *two terms*. Where a Vice President has become President on the death of the President and has served more than two years of the President's term, he shall not be allowed to run for more than one term in addition (1951).

23. Gives the District of Columbia three electoral votes for the election of President and Vice President (1961).

24. *Section 1.* Forbids the United States or any state to abridge or deny any citizen the right to vote for the President or Vice President or for any state representative in Congress because of failure to pay a poll or any other tax. *Section 2.* Gives Congress the power to enforce this article by appropriate legislation (1964).

INDEX

FIRST BOOKS in History, Civics and Geography

HISTORY

Colonial and United States

American Expansion   W Blassingame
American History   H S Commager
American Revolution   R B Morris
The California Gold Rush   W Havighurst
The China Clippers   L D Rich
Cowboys   B Brewster
The Declaration of Independence
The Early Settlers   L D Rich
The Fur Trade   L D Rich
The Gettysburg Address and Second Inau

The Indian Wars   R B Morris
Indians   B Brewster
John F. Kennedy's Inaugural Address
Mount Vernon   G & C Gurney
New World Explorers   L D Rich
The Oregon Trail   W Havighurst
The Panama Canal   P M Markun
Pioneers   W Havighurst
Presidents   H Coy
The Spanish American West   H Castor
The War of 1812   R B Morris
The War with Mexico   H Castor
The White House   L P Jones

HISTORY:

Ancient Bible Lands   C A Robinson
Ancient Crete and Mycenae   C A Robin
Ancient Egypt   C A Robinson
Ancient Greece   C A Robinson
The Ancient Maya   B L Beck
Ancient Mesopotamia and Persia   C A
Ancient Rome   C A Robinson
Archaeology   N B Kubie
Incas   B L Beck
Stone Age Man   A Dickinson
The Vikings   L D Rich

Medieval

The Long Armistice: 1919-1939   L
Medieval Man   D J Sobol
The Mediterranean   G Gottlieb
Palaces   B L Beck
World War I   L L Snyder
World War II   L L Snyder

CIV

Congress   H Coy
The Constitution   R B Morris
Firemen   B Brewster
Holidays   B Burnett
Hospitals   H Coy

CIVICS

International Mail   Henry Hoke
Local Government   J Eichner
Nurses   M Elting
The Supreme Court   H Coy
The United Nations   E Epstein
The World Health Organization   S & B Epstein

...RAPHY

...d States

...h and South America

...Markun

...HY: Europe

...HY: Others